Such Nonsense Indoors

SUCH NONSENSE INDOORS

Poems by

Cora M. Ekwurtzel

Antrim House
Simsbury, Connecticut

Copyright © 2017 by Cora M. Ekwurtzel

Except for short selections reprinted for purposes of
book review, all reproduction rights are reserved.
Requests for permission to replicate should
be addressed to the publisher.

Library of Congress Control Number: 2017937951

ISBN: 978-1-943826-28-5

First Edition, 2017

Printed & bound by Ingram Spark

Book design by Rennie McQuilkin

Front cover photograph by Cheryl Picard

Author photograph by Rennie McQuilkin

Antrim House
860.217.0023
AntrimHouse@comcast.net
www.AntrimHouseBooks.com
21 Goodrich Road, Simsbury, CT 06070

To my loved ones

Table of Contents

With a Book / 3

ALLOWING LIFE TO PASS THROUGH

Substitute / 6
Character / 7
Rod and Reel / 8
Bones / 9
The Bell / 10
The Auction / 11
Wish List / 12
One-third Cup / 13
Purpose / 14
Who Gets to Decide? / 15
The Screen Door / 16
Mid July / 18
One Thousand Pieces / 19
Petals / 20
Flaming Bananas on the Twenty-fourth Floor / 21
Gin and Tonic / 22
Oranges / 23
Peaches / 24
Changeling I / 25
Changeling II / 26
The Bleeding Heart / 27
For Good / 29

GOD WHISPERED IN MY EAR

Rebellion / 32
Turkey Tracks / 33

Goodbye March / 34
Woodbury / 35
Daffodils / 36
The Magnolia / 37
Tulips / 38
Dandelions / 39
Mayflowers / 40
Violets / 41
Fern / 42
Drops / 43
Crab Grass / 44
Night Work / 45
The Hawk / 46
Owl to Owl / 47
Birdie Haiku / 48
Heronry / 49
My Morning Escort / 50
Berries / 51
Mint / 52
Rainbow / 53
Out at Sea / 54
The Hayfield / 55

Acknowledgments / 57
About the Author / 58
About the Book / 59

Such Nonsense Indoors

PRELUDE

With a Book

A woman who walks with a book
tucked in the angle of her arm
holds mystery, a promise
of time spent alone
submerged in study.

She dives into a swirl of ideas
and comes up gasping, sputtering,
gulping knowledge.

Water droplet words cling and
drip in glistening paths
of realization
giving form to thought,
expression to belief.

A woman who reads
swims in a salt sea
buoyed by elements of language.

Her arms stretch long
while cupped hands trap sentences
propelling her mind,
forcing her forward.

She kicks strong legs
in rhythm with her stroke
and glides along
in a competent search
for answers to questions
as infinite as her depth.

ALLOWING LIFE TO PASS THROUGH

Substitute

I wanted a dog.
I got a white mouse
that ran on a noisy wheel
night and day.

I wanted to walk a red dog.
I got a mouse that gave me the creeps
with pink eyes and pink feet.

I wanted a dog with a lolling tongue.
I got a silent, nervous, sniffing rodent
that lived in a glass box.

I wanted a dog to give me the paw.
I got a white mouse
that crept all over me,
like it was doing something wrong.

I wanted a dog to hug and befriend.
I got a mouse that climbed up
one arm and down the other.

I wanted to rest my head on a red dog.
I needed to rest my head on a red dog.
A puny white mouse was
no substitute.

Character

Zip a scarecrow into a green jumpsuit.
Lace on black, shiny, high-topped boots.
Rest thick, wire-rimmed spectacles
on a bulbous red nose.

Place a ukulele in his arms and
listen to him strum and sing
a deep, tuneful baritone.
Join him—he knows all the words.

Curious and analytical,
an engineer and a pilot,
he grew grapes, made wine
and traveled the world.

We stood in his modern kitchen
and marveled at a microwave oven
that boiled water in a wine glass,
leaving the stem cool to touch.

Everyone should have an Uncle Jack,
who stopped by during hard times,
unrolled a few twenties
and gently tucked them into my hand.

Rod and Reel

At night, we sat
at the round kitchen table,
the wood protected by yesterday's news.

We chatted as you set upon
repairing rod and reel,
its mechanism seized by salt and neglect.

Your fingers, grease-stained and familiar
with the choreography of repair,
moved lightly, constantly from tool to task.

I fed you grapefruit,
carefully deveined, pink and succulent,
from the blade of a bone-handled knife.

Bones

My son draws bones late at night.
His assignment (to reproduce skeletal pieces)
requires him to sit for hours
and draw on paper clipped to board.

His movements, rapid and brief—
eye to subject, eye to paper,
hand to charcoal, sketch, rest—
are precise and confident.

Thought directs application of line and shadow.
Mistakes disappear in gummed flakes
brushed off by the artist's hand.

How comforting the sound of paper brushed clean!
Dark to white, old to new,
that whisper of Hope:
Try again.

The Bell

The brass handbell
with a black wooden handle
sat silent on the desk for years,

ignored and dust-covered with cobwebs.
How many times had I passed it by
without noticing its graceful line,
its smooth-turned handle and heft?

So, I picked it up.
And when overturned,
its fig-shaped clapper clanged,
awakening something within me.

I stepped outside and lifted the bell
and rang until my ears stung
from the surge of its sound.

And when my arm ached,
I pumped with the other,
and I pumped and pumped and banged out
a glorious, galloping brass beat.

High over my head, I rang the brass bell
and listened to its pure, clean sound
and felt it pierce and resonate within my breast
until I stood shaking and breathless,
exuberant and exhilarated by my hand
and this once-dormant instrument.

The Auction

Saturday evening is the time
to sell stuff
once precious,
once useful,
once dusted every week,
now boxed on tables.
Potential buyers glance,
shrug, and move on.
The auctioneer's affable style
masks shrewd conviction and
a tense volley of competition
fills the room.
Bland curiosity transforms
to a frenzied quest for possession:
strangers battling over acquisition.
Yesterday, life went on
without the antique brass candlesticks,
the folding glass front,
golden oak barrister's bookcase,
the vintage, one-of-a-kind, impossible-to-replace,
footed, rose-glass candy dish.
Tonight at the auction,
it is unthinkable to go on without them.

Wish List

Lemon-ricotta pancakes,
electric guitar,
apricot jam,
self-driven car.

German shepherd dog,
no glint of fear,
snap my fingers,
inclination made clear.

Lucky winner,
fabulous prize,
spend it all
before my demise.

Grow night vision,
compose a hit song,
predict the future
before it goes wrong.

Frolic with celebrities
every night,
grow feathers and
take flight.

One-third Cup

A kitchen utensil
went missing for a time.
A set of four nesting cups became three,
the gap so evident, distressing me.
Loyalty forbade replacement.
A preposterous search
returned naught.
The spear of blame cast about
a harmonious household
pierced our contentment.
A half cup is easily replaced
by two quarters,
a cup by two halves.
Not so, the one-third cup.
It seeped into my dreams.
The gleaming steel line of it,
the soft curve of its hollow,
the measured exactitude.
One afternoon, the empty sugar bowl
begged refilling.
Paper bag unfurled, base tipped up,
out toppled the one-third cup onto a sugary beach,
its curved line a familiar smile.

Purpose

What are those sticks
holding up your glasses called?
One or the other
is always crooked
or missing a screw.
When you fold them closed
or open them
a fear persists
that one will give out.
And it does.
Wrap some masking tape
or Scotch tape to do the job.
Tape is a bad look
and doesn't quite hold up.
A team of ants could be assembled
To wield the teeny-tiny screwdrivers
to set the teeny-tiny screws.

Who Gets to Decide?

I would like to be the person
who gets to decide
which pictures to
put in the dictionary.
All of those words,
just a few pictures.
Know what a pillory is?
It's worth a diagram:
an unfortunate gentleman
with neck and wrists encased in wood.
You get the picture.
I know what a stepladder looks like.
Don't need a picture
of a tambourine, tarantula or a tick.
Even a child knows a see-saw.
A glengarry?
Ah, that plaid Scottish cap
resembling an inverted canoe.
My father wore one,
on special occasions.

The Screen Door

Wood frames rectangle panes of metal fabric:
hundreds of tiny squares
blend to form a shaded mesh of protection.

The screen door guards
with a hook-and-eye modicum of security,
selectively filtering out bugs, not breezes.

Through it,
heated voices travel
on the night air of summer:
a satisfying slam punctuates
a statement with finality.

Moths bat the screen:
their persistent fluttering,
futile and absurd, continues
until the light is extinguished,
their attraction abated.

From a safe venue
behind it,
I watch a summer storm,
feeling the atmospheric pressure drop.
The wild wind and rain
electrify my senses
and thrill my soul.

The screen door swings,
allowing life to pass through.
Springed hinges pluck
a familiar twang
to the come-and-go rhythm
of summer.

Mid July

The raspberry patch requires
a moderate amount of work
to keep it cultivated, weed free,
and fruit-bearing.

Throughout the spring
we stoop low to grasp stubborn weeds,
cull the old hollow canes
and snip the new ones.

Until mid-July, we wait,
knowing that soon
the canes will droop heavy
with fat red berries

The turkeys know too.
At dawn we hear the scramble
as Tom leads his hen
and brood of eight.

One Thousand Pieces

A rainy day at the lake
suspended outdoor play.
A wobbly card table
and a faded box of shapes
challenged to hold our attention.

One thousand pieces.
And somehow we summoned
the patience and concentration
required to put them together.

We gathered and sorted and fit and refit,
temporarily distracted from our forlorn place.
Our reward, a dim image of a generic location,
a fancy castle in Germany or some such scene.

Seen from the damp shelter of the porch
the tantalizing lake paused to refill.
Its dappled surface was a blurry silhouette
forbidden until the summer storm subsided.
We couldn't wait.

Petals

A trip to the market
with the sun roof open
gave opportunity for loose,
lacy, apple blossom petals
to flutter in and land
on my lap.

Flaming Bananas on the Twenty-fourth Floor

We simply pushed a button
ascending to the Stargazer Casino.
Glass and steel—
ostentatious luxury
in the Connecticut woods.

We simply settled
on a sofa
luxuriating by the hearth.

Yes, of course,
simply set our dessert aflame
serve it bubbling,
melt our expectations.

Gin and Tonic

In the summer I drink gin and tonic:
effervescent clarity on ice.

Cold bubbles pop and burst
to moisten my lips and nose

with the lush,
verdant flavor of lime and juniper.

Sunset and shade trees,
birdsong and breezes,

thought and melody,
gin and tonic.

Oranges

Is it coincidence
that a slice of orange
is shaped like a smile?

When the pocked leather peel
is stripped from the fruit
in ragged puzzle pieces,
fingers are perfumed
with exotic spicy oil.

The globe
sections naturally
for sharing.

Tiny sacs,
their fragile membranes
filled with sweet nectar,
burst open with
each bite.

Is it coincidence
that a slice of orange
is shaped like a smile?

Peaches
(a lesson)

The peach tree in my neighbor's yard,
grew for years unnoticed until
one day he pointed and said, "Take some."

We circled it in an odd, spastic dance,
stooping and stretching to grasp
each ripe one.

His breath, caught and imprisoned
in ancient, noisy passages
came out hitched:
"This... is... a... good... one,"
he said and repeated.

The fruit looked small and pale,
spotted and unripe to me.
"The whimsy of an old man," I thought.

We sat at the picnic table
and reached into the bulging brown bag.
One after another we peeled and ate the peaches,
intoxicated by tender sweetness.

Changeling I

In late October the spirits are released,
some good and some the other.
Mischief and trickery skim the surface
of sinister canyons beneath.

The underbelly of a bridge
traps moisture and grows dank,
harbors desperate characters
leering and gnawing for a fix:

a place where an insignificant woman
exchanged an eight-pound burden
for a new baby, snatched from her crib;
parents never heard a sound.

Not a quarter hour had passed
before fate crossed the line.
The troll baby, putrid and wheezing,
awakened a sleeping mother.

In the darkness, the swaddling
unfolded to reveal a gurgling, demonic form
mewling, with gnarled limbs and sunken chest
eager for a mother's sustaining breast.

Changeling II

The new mother's milk
involuntarily spurted from generous breasts
and the mother ignored the apparition,
blaming it on hormones and sleeplessness.

She scooped up the wheezing infant
and sank into the familiar rocking chair,
mother and baby settling into the ancient
reciprocal repose of give and take.

Lulled by the mother's soothing kisses
and fueled by the plentiful, life-giving milk,
the troll baby grasped the mother's finger
and an unexpected metamorphosis began.

Cell by cell the baby regenerated
as she drank the sweet sustenance.
While the drowsy mother snoozed,
grotesque transformed to radiance.

When the infant had drunk its fill,
its belly sated and content,
mother returned her to the crib
to dream baby dreams of belonging.

The Bleeding Heart

Such profound emotion is inspired
by the perennial bleeding heart—
delicate, fragile beauty
suspended in pink lanterns of melancholy
arc towards the earth
as if stooped by a
long-held burden of sorrow.

For whom does the bleeding heart grieve?
Does it lock a teardrop of dew
in its milky glass chamber for each of us

who have known the sting
of unrequited love,
the sorrow of goodbye,
the insane longing to be held
in the tender embrace
of arms that no longer exist,

to see a face,
hear a voice
that causes the heart
to quicken
by some instinctive response,
to rest your head
on a breast of contentment,
the heartbeat and breath
a deeply familiar synchrony.

Simply the sight of this flower
reawakens our dormant sorrow,
for love leaves us,
life leaves us,
though loss is honorable proof
of a life well-lived.

For Good

Summer is like a bad boyfriend.
He rides in on the slipstream of spring
and warms you, burnishes your skin,
temporarily blinds you
and you become silly with heat.

Oh yes, your blossoms open.
Oh yes, your senses ignite.
Oh yes, when the corn ripens
you sleep naked, stripped of every convention,
the gauze of modesty lifted.

And then he gives an early sign,
the days shorten, here and there a leaf turns red.
Desperate to keep him, you cling tighter
and beg, shameless, frantic for possession.
But, Autumn has already claimed him
and turned his gaze for good.

GOD WHISPERED IN MY EAR

Rebellion

Although I was surrounded by opulence—
a grand staircase, crystal chandeliers
and intellectuals seated on chintz—
what impressed me was outside the window,
where moss clumps clung to cracks
in a huge boulder
fuzzy and brave and
unconcerned with the nonsense indoors.
Its green was pure rebellion
on this February afternoon in Connecticut.

Turkey Tracks

In February, the snowfall was frequent.
White covered every corner of the field,
softening the terrain into mounds and drifts.

Wind gusts flew up from the valley,
causing snow ghosts to lift their skirts
and dance like dervishes,
raising their arms and swirling
in graceful pirouettes.

And between the frosty dancers
walked wild turkeys, stepping gingerly
across the frozen field,
their small crimson heads bobbing,
their long necks outstretched and
searching...

Buffeted by layers of brown feathers,
the reflection of muted sunlight
glinted with alluring iridescence,
illuminating their winter beauty.

The snow dancers continued,
oblivious to the birds (or so it seemed)
and where the dancing footsteps fell,
small patches of green grass were revealed.
The turkeys quickly gathered
and devoured every blade.

Goodbye March

Day after day of marginal weather
gives way to windy days
to mix up the mess.
March, the laggard,
serves up winter's leftovers,
failing to convince us it is worth the wait.

Woodbury

A native plant nursery
set deep in the woods
hosts bumblebees on Earth Day.
A small painted turtle
climbs a rock
to find the sun.
Too early for leaf-out,
the woods are naked,
the brown floor exposed.
Stones pop here and there.
A few spectacular blooms
like miracles
of color and scent
line the rough path.
Winter shifts into spring.

Daffodils

"Hey you!" wave the daffodils,
those noisy, honking geese
in ruffled, yellow bonnets.

"Wake up!" they cry,
announcing spring's arrival
with their brass trumpet's blare.

"Join us!" they call from
congenial clusters, proclaiming
Spring.

The Magnolia

A silent breeze stirs the magnolia from sleep,
her tender blossoms, pink and white,
bob up, down, side to side in graceful stagger.

Late day sunlight kisses each petal
and they shimmer
in a collective, riotous celebration.

I want to close my eyes,
bury my face in their cool, damp centers,
and make them my own.

Tulips

The tulip doesn't bother with flirtation.
It beckons with no nuance.
Every color is a boast.
The bawdy red makes no apologies.
The majestic purple dares me.
The blinding yellow says,
"Take me as I am."
And I do,
snip each pencil stem,
capture each brash character
to fill a vase with life.

Dandelions

The dandelions appear in the morning,
as if bright yellow drops of paint
had been spilled from the heavens,

or as if the just-up sun were melting,
and drip, drip, dropping
golden dots
in haphazard perfusion.

The flower heads'
shaggy yellow whiskers,
beaming optimism,
beckon children
who tug at pliant stems
and present to mothers
their first awkward, drooping
bouquets of innocence.

The tender, forked leaf
grows bitter with age,
goes from gilded flower
to translucent orb
whose spectral globe of
exquisite fragility

is dispensed to the air
by a child's determined puff
to alight and set down,
and begin again.

Mayflowers

Bow deep
and greet the cheery mayflowers!

Powdered lavender-on-white
petals of perfect symmetry

fuse to a tiny center
of sunny yellow.

Intolerant of winter's lot,
they shiver from the
slightest breeze.

Clustered together,
they wait… and wait…
until fickle April passes,

then rise on valiant thready stems
to the silent command of spring

and proclaim the month of May
be held in their diminutive sway.

Violets

Violets, as common as pennies,
grow along the garden wall:

purple and white florets
protected by emerald leaves
snuggle between cool, brown stones.

Fern

The fronds rose like open arms
from the the strong root center,
a mass of symmetrical triangle shapes,
a green so alive
I wanted to wring myself out,
compress myself
into a small round plug,
drop into the open center
and rest below the cool, green stems.

Drops

Outside my kitchen window
the leafless trumpet vines
are an unremarkable tangle.

From one of them, rod-straight,
hang twelve clear raindrops
perfectly spaced and suspended
like thoughts,
uninterrupted.

Crab Grass

Recently, I heard that crab grass
does not propagate like the others.

The flat, sharp spears *themselves*
regenerate,
when sliced by the lawnmower blade.

Fresh clippings burst across the yard
and settle in,
infuriating every green-carpeted suburbanite.

Cheers for Crab Grass
who is not outdone
by chemicals, machinery, or spite!

Night Work

A walk along the old, abandoned canal bank
during winter is arduous.
Smooth pavement steps
are slowed by snow-covered oak leaves.
Sure-footed becomes the opposite.

The water flow slows as well,
the surge arrested by
a raggedy patch of branches and leaves.
Not an indiscriminate
collection of nature's refuse,
but an purposeful,
cleverly disguised baffle.

Saplings are chisel-cut.
Foot-long spears poke through the snow.
Ironwood, birch and oak all felled,
bark stripped, gnawed into manageable
lengths and dragged down the bank.

Buried in the mud, butt upstream
and anchored by ingenuity,
the beaver dam grows each night
reducing the stream's rush
to a trickle.

The Hawk

I am the hawk
who alone flies high,
my silhouette a mere speck
soaring in blue,
my dizzy, feathered flight
hollow-boned and effortless.

I am the hawk
who alone flies low,
circling bare branches,
searching for what fulfills
and what sustains
a restless spirit.

I am the hawk
who alone is perched
on a strong tree branch,
contemplating the cold river water
that flows, cresting between steep banks.

I am a patient sentinel,
unobtrusively observing,
silently gathering wisdom
from what passes below.

Owl to Owl

Listen for the owls
at the quietest time,
their vocalization
for each other,
not our ears.
We have no word for it—
neither a "hoot" nor a "whoo-whoo."
Nothing human compares.
Soft-edged,
from a deep place,
baffled by feathers and bone.
Appealing, yet unsettling.
Alluring, but disturbing.
Inviting, but risky.
Familiar, yet exotic.
Plaintive and haunting,
it implores
sleepy self-examination,
with only the stars
and other night creatures as witness.

Birdie Haiku

The Chickadee

The chickadee's song
is her own name
repeated and repeated.

The Cardinal

In a scarlet robe
the reticent cardinal
hides amidst brambles

The Owl

I know where the owl
sleeps during the day.
Shhh, it's a secret.

The Blue Jay

The sassy jay wears
a fine, feathered tuxedo
blue, bold and bossy

Heronry

I make excuses to pedal over or drive by.
That neighborhood is my idea of moving up.
Like 60's fashion models they arrive in late March,
Manhattan-thin, all bone and feathers,
minimalist, monochrome elegance.

On windy nights the nests sway,
precarious, elite community
of prehistoric tree dwellers
minding their business.

And me, the voyeur with binoculars
risking limb to stand on the shoulder
of a country road to marvel
at dead trees in standing water,
topped by tattered stick nests
with a few lightweight characters
hanging around.

The herons, hunted to near extinction
for feathers to adorn women's hats,
nest in tree tops
in simple, grand style.

My Morning Escort

Half asleep,
turn right and head out.
When I cross the stream,
a great blue heron
surprises me.
Beneath the leafy canopy
at eye level,
close enough for me
to hear its wingbeats,
my morning escort
flies long and low.
Not a flash nor a quick sighting,
but a quarter-mile escort.
Just us
starting our day,
together.

Berries

Would it sound foolish
if I confided
that the best moment of summer
I spent alone
early one morning,
picking berries for breakfast?

Drowsy light filtered through
morning mist,
illuminating green leaves
and red berry-clusters.

My fingers parted
leaves moist with dew
and were pierced by
thorns protecting ripe fruit.

I sampled berries
as I picked,
each one tender and sweet,
full-flavored and fresh.

The mockingbird sang
her erratic, borrowed song,
sunlight strengthened,
and God whispered
in my ear,

Mint

When poverty visited
I picked wild mint
that grew along the roadside

and tucked a green leaf
under my tongue
for reassurance

and waited
for its quieting flavor
to soothe my longing
and sustain me

until it slowly dissolved
into tiny shreds
and then disintegrated
into nothing.

Rainbow

Yesterday, I saw a rainbow—
not an arch of nebulous beginning or end
but a stout, vertical shaft of misty color
linking treetops to clouds.

I stared at this odd wonder
connecting earth and sky
until the colored mist faded,

leaving my heart full of
pride?
gratitude?
I still cannot tell.

Out At Sea

Out on the water, all is horizontal—
no trees with their sturdy, deeply rooted trunks,
no buildings with their excavated foundations,
just us, in a small boat with the air in our faces
and the sea salt smells.
But if we are alone, who leaves the imprints
on the water's surface?
The wind skitters here and there, her skirts brushing by,
big fish, lured by small silver flashes
rise up, break through,
and the swells, the water itself breathing
huge sighs of relief,
the deep heaving cadence of slumber
or the peaceful rise and fall
of a woman lulled in the arms of a loved one.
The horizon does not separate
Earth from sky, right from wrong, good from bad.
And there we sit, in our little boat, a part of it all,
buoyed by the sea, its elements
making up our very breath,
our miniscule weight
graciously accepted and anchored by gravity,
all at no charge.
For now, we are the ones who belong to both
above and below, between both worlds,
the pinnacle and the depth.
The water laps the stern like a wet-tongued dog
happy to see us.

The Hayfield

From a distance the hayfield looks
like a huge sheet
of billowing green fabric
set out to dry
in the soft breezes of June.

Between slim wire stalks of hay
live the wildflowers,
volunteering but not boasting
of their colorful, demure beauty.

Walk through the hayfield and
listen to the dry seed heads
rasp as you wander through
thigh-high grass;

feel the coarse brushing friction
on legs and hands.
Pick a slender stalk to
clamp between teeth, and
taste the sweet subtle
flavor of winter fodder;

watch the wind-blown
patterns swirling
through the field,
surrounding you
with rippling, weaving
iridescent shades of green.

Acknowledgments

I would like to thank the late Larry Gilman of Westminster School, who taught me to understand the value of my early poems; and also Westminster's Michael Cervas for publishing my poems in *The Martlet*.

I am grateful to Rennie McQuiliken for his patience and guidance through the process of producing this book, and to Cheryl Picard for her perfect cover photo.

I also thank my lifelong friend, Luanne Rice, for sharing her writing knowledge and expertise.

I have deep gratitude for the gift of my best friend, Joanie Wain, host of my first poetry reading, who swims along with me in every sea.

Finally, I thank my husband, Stephen Ekwurtzel, who keeps the fires and anchors the stone.

Cora Ekwurtzel grew up in Massachusetts and moved to a farm in Granby, Connecticut, where she raised her family and still lives with her husband, Steve. In the summer, you will pass her on the road bicycling to Congamond Lake for a swim or boating. In the winter, you will find her ice skating or cozied up, reading a slim volume of poetry by the fire. She has a motorcycle license, a boating license and a nursing license. An avid gardener, she wrote her first poem when inspired by picking ripe tomatoes in the hot August sun. Her engagement with the world of nature is often reflected in her poetry. A lightning strike annealed her, and she tells the story with humor, amazement and gratitude for life.

This book is set in Garamond Premier Pro, which had its genesis in 1988 when type-designer Robert Slimbach visited the Plantin-Moretus Museum in Antwerp, Belgium, to study its collection of Claude Garamond's metal punches and typefaces. During the mid-fifteen hundreds, Garamond—a Parisian punch-cutter—produced a refined array of book types that combined an unprecedented degree of balance and elegance, for centuries standing as the pinnacle of beauty and practicality in type-founding. Slimbach has created an entirely new interpretation based on Garamond's designs and on compatible italics cut by Robert Granjon, Garamond's contemporary.

To order additional copies of this book
or other Antrim House titles, contact the publisher at

Antrim House
21 Goodrich Rd., Simsbury, CT 06070
860.217.0023, AntrimHouse@comcast.net
or the house website (www.AntrimHouseBooks.com).

•

On the house website
in addition to information on books
you will find sample poems, upcoming events,
and a "seminar room" featuring supplemental biography,
notes, images, poems, reviews, and
writing suggestions.

CPSIA information can be obtained
at www.ICGtesting.com
Printed in the USA
BVOW08s1429181217
503103BV00004B/557/P